STUL

MW01252361

THE GOSPEL ACCORDING TO
MATTHEW

Little Rock Scripture Study Staff

LITTLE ROCK SCRIPTURE STUDY

*A ministry of the Diocese of Little Rock
in partnership with Liturgical Press*

Dear Friends in Christ,

The Bible comes to us as both a gift and an opportunity. It is a gift of God who loves us enough to communicate with us. The only way to enjoy the gift is to open and savor it. The Bible is also an opportunity to actually meet God who is present in the stories, teachings, people, and prayers that fill its pages.

I encourage you to open your Bibles in anticipation that God will do something good in your life. I encourage you to take advantage of the opportunity to meet God in prayer, study, and small-group discussion.

Little Rock Scripture Study offers materials that are simple to use, and a method that has been tested by time. The questions in this study guide will direct your study, help you to understand the passages you are reading, and challenge you to relate the Scriptures to your own life experiences.

Allow the Word of God to form you as a disciple of the Lord Jesus. Accept the challenge to be "transformed by the renewal of your mind" (Romans 12:2). Above all, receive God's Word as his gift, and act upon it.

Sincerely in Christ,

✚ J. Peter Sartain

✚ J. Peter Sartain
Bishop of Little Rock

Sacred Scripture

"The Church has always venerated the divine Scriptures just as she venerates the body of the Lord, since from the table of both the word of God and of the body of Christ she unceasingly receives and offers to the faithful the bread of life, especially in the sacred liturgy. She has always regarded the Scriptures together with sacred tradition as the supreme rule of faith, and will ever do so. For, inspired by God and committed once and for all to writing, they impart the word of God Himself without change, and make the voice of the Holy Spirit resound in the words of the prophets and apostles. Therefore, like the Christian religion itself, all the preaching of the Church must be nourished and ruled by sacred Scripture. For in the sacred books, the Father who is in heaven meets His children with great love and speaks with them; and the force and power in the word of God is so great that it remains the support and energy of the Church, the strength of faith for her sons, the food of the soul, the pure and perennial source of spiritual life."

Vatican II, Dogmatic Constitution on Divine Revelation, no. 21.

INTERPRETATION OF SACRED SCRIPTURE

"Since God speaks in sacred Scripture through men in human fashion, the interpreter of sacred Scripture, in order to see clearly what God wanted to communicate to us, should carefully investigate what meaning the sacred writers really intended, and what God wanted to manifest by means of their words.

"Those who search out the intention of the sacred writers must, among other things, have regard for 'literary forms.' For truth is proposed and expressed in a variety of ways, depending on whether a text is history of one kind or another, or whether its form is that of prophecy, poetry, or some other type of speech. The interpreter must investigate what meaning the sacred writer intended to express and actually expressed in particular circumstances as he used contemporary literary forms in accordance with the situation of his own time and culture. For the correct understanding of what the sacred author wanted to assert, due attention must be paid to the customary and characteristic styles of perceiving, speaking, and narrating which prevailed at the time of the sacred writer, and to the customs men normally followed in that period in their everyday dealings with one another."

Vatican II, Dogmatic Constitution on Divine Revelation, no. 12.

Instructions

MATERIALS FOR THE STUDY

This Study Guide: The Gospel According to Matthew

Bible: The New American Bible with Revised New Testament or The New Jerusalem Bible is recommended. Paraphrased editions are discouraged as they offer little if any help when facing difficult textual questions. Choose a Bible you feel free to write in or underline.

Commentary: The New Collegeville Bible Commentary, volume 1, *The Gospel According to Matthew* by Barbara E. Reid, O.P. (Liturgical Press) is used with this study. The abbreviation for this commentary, NCBC-NT volume 1, and the assigned pages are found at the beginning of each lesson.

ADDITIONAL MATERIALS

Bible Dictionary: *The Dictionary of the Bible* by John L. McKenzie (Simon & Schuster) is highly recommended as a reference.

Notebook: A notebook may be used for lecture notes and your personal reflections.

WEEKLY LESSONS

Lesson 1—Matt 1–2
Lesson 2—Matt 3–5

Lesson 3—Matt 6–8
Lesson 4—Matt 9–12
Lesson 5—Matt 13–16
Lesson 6—Matt 17–19
Lesson 7—Matt 20–22
Lesson 8—Matt 23–25
Lesson 9—Matt 26–28

YOUR DAILY PERSONAL STUDY

The first step is prayer. Open your heart and mind to God. Reading Scripture is an opportunity to listen to God who loves you. Pray that the same Holy Spirit who guided the formation of Scripture will inspire you to correctly understand what you read and empower you to make what you read a part of your life.

The next step is commitment. Daily spiritual food is as necessary as food for the body. This study is divided into daily units. Schedule a regular time and place for your study, as free from distractions as possible. Allow about twenty minutes a day. Make it a daily appointment with God.

As you begin each lesson read the assigned chapters of Scripture found at the beginning of each lesson, the footnotes in your Bible, and then the indicated pages of the commentary. This preparation will give you an overview of the entire lesson and help you to appreciate the context of individual passages.

As you reflect on Scripture, ask yourself these four questions:

1. *What does the Scripture passage say?*
   Read the passage slowly and reflectively. Use your imagination to picture the scene or enter into it.

2. *What does the Scripture passage mean?*
   Read the footnotes and the commentary to help you understand what the sacred writers intended and what God wanted to communicate by means of their words.

3. *What does the Scripture passage mean to me?*
   Meditate on the passage. God's Word is living and powerful. What is God saying to you today? How does the Scripture passage apply to your life today?

4. *What am I going to do about it?*
    Try to discover how God may be challenging you in this passage. An encounter with God contains a challenge to know God's will and follow it more closely in daily life.

THE QUESTIONS ASSIGNED FOR EACH DAY

Read the questions and references for each day. The questions are designed to help you listen to God's Word and to prepare you for the weekly small-group discussion.

Some of the questions can be answered briefly and objectively by referring to the Bible references and the commentary *(What does the passage say?)*. Some will lead you to a better understanding of how the Scriptures apply to the Church, sacraments, and society *(What does the passage mean?)*. Some questions will invite you to consider how God's Word challenges or supports you in your relationships with God and others *(What does the passage mean to me?)*. Finally, the questions will lead you to examine your actions in light of Scripture *(What am I going to do about it?)*.

Write your responses in this study guide or in a notebook to help you clarify and organize your thoughts and feelings.

THE WEEKLY SMALL-GROUP MEETING

The weekly small-group sharing is the heart of the Little Rock Scripture Study Program. Participants gather in small groups to share the results of praying, reading, and reflecting on Scripture and on the assigned questions. The goal of the discussion is for group members to be strengthened and nourished individually and as a community through sharing how God's Word speaks to them and affects their daily lives. The daily study questions will guide the discussion; it is not necessary to discuss all the questions.

All members share the responsibility of creating an atmosphere of loving support and trust in the group by respecting the opinions and experiences of others, and by affirming and encouraging one another. The simple shared prayer which begins and ends each small group meeting also helps create the open and trusting environment in which group members can share their faith deeply and grow in the study of God's Word.

A distinctive feature of this program is its emphasis on and trust in God's presence working in and through each member. Sharing responses to God's presence in the Word and in others can bring about remarkable growth and transformation.

THE WRAP-UP LECTURE

The lecture is designed to develop and clarify the themes of each lesson. It is not intended to be the focus of the group's discussion. For this reason, the lecture always occurs *after* the small group discussion. If several small groups meet at one time, the groups may gather in a central location to listen to the lecture.

Lectures may be presented by a local speaker. They are also available in audio form on cassette or CD, and in visual form on cassette or DVD.

Matthew I–2

NCBC-NT VOLUME I, PAGES 5–21

Day I

1. What do you most hope for from your study of Matthew's Gospel?

2. What aspects of Matthew's Gospel support the scholarly opinion that its author was a Jewish Christian, writing for an audience that was also primarily Jewish Christian?

3. a) Why is 85 A.D. considered a good approximate date for the completion of the Gospel according to Matthew?

   b) Why is it considered likely that Matthew's Gospel was written for a prosperous urban community?

Day 2

4. a) Besides Mary, who were the women identified by Matthew in Jesus' genealogy (1:3, 5-6)?

   b) What special notes about Jesus' ancestry do they bring to the genealogy? (See Gen 38; Josh 2; Ruth 1–4; 2 Sam 11.)

5. What were probably some of Matthew's reasons for writing down Jesus' genealogy?

6. How does what we learn of Joseph in Matthew show him to be a righteous man (1:18-25)? (See 2:13-23.)

Day 3

7. Joseph took direction from his dreams (1:20). Have you ever had a dream that you feel said something important to you? (See 2:13, 19, 22; also Acts 2:17.)

8. Why is the Greek Septuagint translation of Isaiah 7:14 of key importance to Matthew's proclamation of Jesus' birth to the virgin named Mary (1:23)?

9. Emmanuel is a name for Jesus that means, "God is with us" (1:23). When have you felt in a special way that God was with you?

Day 4

10. Who or what were the magi (2:1)?

11. How does Matthew use the visit of the magi to prepare his readers for the inclusion of the Gentiles in the mission of the Church (2:1-12)? (See 8:11; 28:18-20.)

12. The magi followed a star to find Jesus (2:2, 9-11). What has guided you in your journey to Jesus?

Day 5

13. How does the flight to Egypt help Matthew create a special link to Jesus' identity (2:13-15)? (See Hos 11:1.)

14. What might Herod's motives be for attempting to slaughter the child Jesus (2:16)?

15. How does the prophet Jeremiah's depiction of Rachael weeping for her children (Jer 31:15-17) paint a different picture from Matthew's use of it (2:18)?

Day 6

16. Why does Joseph take his family to Galilee instead of returning to Judea (2:19-23)?

17. Does Matthew regard Bethlehem as the original home of Joseph and Mary (2:1, 21-23)?

18. For what reasons might Jesus' identification as a Nazorean be treated as a fulfillment of prophecy in Matthew (2:23)? (See Isa 11:1; Judg 13:5-7; Num 6:1-21.)

Matthew 3–5

NCBC-NT VOLUME 1, PAGES 21–41

Day 1

1. Besides Mary and Joseph, recall something from last week's study about the significant role others played in the circumstances surrounding Jesus' birth (1:1-17; 2:1-12, 16).

2. a) What is the theme of John the Baptist's preaching (3:2)?

   b) Why does Matthew prefer "kingdom of heaven" to Mark and Luke's use of the phrase "kingdom of God" (3:2)? (See Mark 1:15; Luke 4:43.)

3. Are there people today whom you might identify as a "voice of one crying out in the desert" (3:3)?

Day 2

4. What are some important details found in the commentary concerning who the Pharisees and Sadducees were (3:7)?

5. How does Matthew's account of Jesus' baptism attempt to explain why the Messiah sought baptism from John (3:11-17)?

6. How does the temptation of Jesus (4:1-11) echo the experience of Israel following the Exodus (Exod 16:1-10)? (See Heb 3:7-10; Ps 95:7-10.)

Day 3

7. If even the devil can quote Scripture, how can we know when it is being used or interpreted correctly (4:5-6)? (See 1 Cor 12:27-30; Eph 4:11-15; James 1:22-25; 2 Pet 2:1.)

8. What does the call of the first disciples teach about the obligations of discipleship (4:18-22)?

9. a) Identify three major elements of Jesus' initial ministry (4:23)?

   b) What aspect of Jesus' ministry seems to have attracted the most attention (4:24)?

Day 4

10. What is the importance of both the location of Jesus' sermon and his posture in delivering it (5:1)? (See Exod 18:13; 19:3, 16-20.)

11. a) Which of the beatitudes (5:1-12) seems most important to you? Why?

    b) Which of the beatitudes (5:1-12) seems in shortest supply today?

12. In what ways does your faith community strive to be a city on a mountain, a light that cannot be hidden (5:14-16)?

Day 5

13. Why might Jesus' attitude toward the Mosaic Law be of special importance in Matthew's community (5:17-20)?

14. How does Jesus' teaching about anger actually help prevent breaking the commandment against killing (5:21-26)? (See Exod 20:13.)

15. Can you recall a time when an act of reconciliation saved an important relationship in your life (5:23-24)?

Day 6

16. If we are not to take literally this teaching about dismembering parts of our body that we think are leading us into sin, how are we supposed to understand it (5:29-30)?

17. a) How has the Catholic Church attempted to honor the teachings of Jesus concerning divorce and remarriage (5:31-32) and yet also respond to the reality of divorce among the faithful? (See Luke 16:18.)

    b) What does the commentary say about the conditions for an "unlawful" marriage in Matthew's community (5:32)?

18. Have you witnessed or experienced someone practicing the teachings of Jesus concerning responding to evil or those who mean harm (5:38-48)?

Matthew 6–8

NCBC-NT VOLUME 1, PAGES 41–54

Day 1

1. Recalling last week's lesson, which of the beatitudes would you be most likely to ask God to prosper in your own life (5:2-11)?

2. Does declaring charitable giving for tax relief violate the spirit of Jesus' teaching on giving in secret (6:1-4)?

3. When we ask God for "our daily bread," what are we asking for (6:11)? (See Prov 30:8; Acts 2:46.)

Day 2

4. When you think of treasures stored in heaven, do you think of them more as a reward for good deeds and behavior or the good character that has been formed by living according to Jesus' teachings (6:19-21)?

5. It seems that some pursuit of money is an economic necessity. How does one make certain that God is the one being served and still provide for one's self, family, and others (6:24)?

6. How would the lifestyle of early Christian communities as described by Luke in Acts 2:44-45 have contributed to their ability to live without worry for the needs of tomorrow (6:25-32)?

Day 3

7. How does admitting and attending to one's own spiritual shortcomings make someone more fit to address the faults of others (7:5)?

8. How could those who have not experienced receiving good gifts from a parent actually learn to trust God as a giver of good gifts (7:7-11)?

9. What special or random act of kindness might you plan to exercise this week (7:12)?

Day 4

10. What concern might there be today for "false prophets" and what "fruit" might you recognize them by (7:15-20)? (See Deut 13:2-5; Jer 23:16-17, 25-28.)

11. The crowds were astonished at Jesus' teaching because he spoke with authority. What do you find most astonishing about his teaching (7:28-29)? (See Mark 1:21-22.)

12. a) Cleansing a leper meant more than just healing the disease. What else would be restored to a leper after a healing (8:1-4)? (See Lev 13:45-46.)

   b) In our culture, whom do we treat like the lepers of biblical times? (See Num 5:1-4.)

Day 5

13. How did the centurion demonstrate unusual faith, but also, perhaps, a concern for Jesus' ritual purity (8:5-10)?

14. In the account of Jesus healing Peter's mother-in-law, what is there to suggest that he was also calling her to discipleship (8:14-15)? (See Matt 9:9; 20:28; Acts 6:2-6; also, see Rom 15:25; 1 Cor 16:15, where the root word for "ministry" is the same as for the word "serve.")

15. Why might Jesus' healing ministry have attracted some with less than perfect motives to follow him (Matt 8:16-22)? (See John 2:23-25; Acts 8:9-24.)

Day 6

16. What are some meanings associated with the title "Son of Man" by which Jesus refers to himself for the first time in 8:20? (See Dan 7:13-14; Matt 9:6; 10:23; 11:19; 12:40; 13:41; 17:9.)

17. How do some of the Psalms shed light on the question the disciples ask concerning Jesus' ability to calm the storm (8:23-27)? (See Ps 65:8; 89:10; 107:28-29.)

18. In what ways might today's followers of Christ show his power over evil (8:28-34) on the margins of our society?

Matthew 9–12

NCBC-NT VOLUME 1, PAGES 54–73

Day 1

1. What is something that stands out to you from last week's lesson about Jesus as either a teacher or a healer?

2. How would healing a paralytic demonstrate Jesus' authority to forgive sins (9:1-6)? (See John 9:2.)

3. a) Why was the company Jesus kept at his meals of such concern (9:9-11)? (See 11:19.)

   b) How might Jesus' response to John's disciples concerning fasting have added to that concern (9:14-15)? (See 8:11; Isa 25:6-8; 62:5.)

Day 2

4. How does the way Jesus compares his teaching with wine and wineskins in Matthew (9:17) differ from Mark's account (Mark 2:22)?

5. How does your commentary note some of the similarities between the suffering of the two women Jesus restores to health and Jesus' own passion (9:18-25)? (See Matt 27–28.)

6. The title "Son of David," by which the blind men address Jesus (9:27), is found eight other times in Matthew (1:1, 20; 12:23; 15:22; 20:30, 31; 21:9, 15). What is its significance?

Day 3

7. How does Jesus' compassion for the crowds recall Moses' concern for Israel (9:36)? (See Num 27:17-18.)

8. Why does Jesus tell his disciples that they must be "shrewd as serpents and simple as doves" (10:16)?

9. a) Have you ever felt prejudice, discrimination, or been persecuted because of your beliefs (10:22-25)?

   b) Are there people with religious identities in your area who face some form of persecution or discrimination for their beliefs?

Day 4

10. Why would Jesus claim that he did not come to bring peace, but a sword (10:34)? (See 5:9, 38-48; 26:52 for Jesus' teachings on peace; see 4:21-22; 8:21-22 for other pertinent examples.)

11. What is the biblical context that would have enabled John the Baptist to fully understand Jesus' response to his question (11:2-6)? (See Isa 26:19; 29:18-19, and especially 35:4-6; 61:1.)

12. a) How does Jesus contrast the public reception of John the Baptist's ministry with his own (11:16-19)?

    b) What in their ministries would be responsible for such responses (3:1-10; 9:9-10, 14-15)? (See Luke 1:15.)

Day 5

13. How does Jesus' prayer of thanksgiving in 11:25-26 reflect the beatitudes of 5:3-9?

14. Considering all the demands and consequences Jesus assigns to discipleship (6:24; 8:19-22; 10:34-38), what do you think makes Jesus' yoke "easy," his burden "light" (11:30)?

15. Why might Jesus' claim to have authority to rule on questions about Sabbath activities have been a bigger concern than what he or his disciples actually did on the Sabbath (12:1-14)? (See 7:28-29; 9:6; and Exod 20:8.)

Day 6

16. How does the quotation from Isaiah concerning the chosen servant help explain why Jesus warned those he had healed not to make him known (12:15-21)? (See Isa 42:1-3.)

17. What do you understand about why offending the Spirit was such a great offense (12:22-33)?

18. What are the distinguishing characteristics of those who belong to the family of Jesus (12:46-50)? (See Mark 3:31-35; Luke 8:19-21.)

Matthew 13–16

NCBC-NT VOLUME 1, PAGES 73–90

Day 1

1. What is something you studied Jesus saying or doing in last week's lesson that continues to attract your attention, raise questions, or move you in some way?

2. What have the disciples seen and heard that the righteous and prophets of other ages longed to see and hear, but did not (13:16-17)?

3. What would you consider authentic signs that the seeds Jesus calls "the word of the kingdom" have sprouted and grown in a hearer (13:18-23)? (See 5:2-11; Rom 14:17; Gal 5:22-23.)

Day 2

4. How might the parable of the weeds and the wheat encourage patience in accepting other people (13:24-30)? (See 1 Cor 4:5.)

5. How could Jesus' use of parables be compared to the woman's use of yeast (13:33)?

6. Pick a favorite parable or story with images told by Jesus and recorded in Matthew. Explain what it speaks to you and why it is important to you (13:1-50). (See also 7:24-27; 18:12-14; 18:23-35; 20:1-16; 21:28-43; 22:2-14; 24:45-51; 25:1-13, and 25:14-30.)

Day 3

7. The wise scribe knows the value of both the old and the new (13:52-53). Who or what have been the sources of this wisdom for you?

8. Matthew says Jesus "did not" work many miracles because of their lack of faith (13:58), but Mark says he "was not able" to do them (Mark 6:5). Why might Matthew have chosen to word his account in this way?

9. Jesus' feeding of the five thousand echoes themes from the Exodus and the life of the prophet Elisha (14:13-21). (See Exod 16; Num 11:31-35; 2 Kgs 4:42-44.) How do those themes shed light on Jesus' intentions in feeding them?

Day 4

10. In what ways does Matthew's account of Jesus walking on water show Jesus to be like God (14:22-33)? (See Exod 3:14; Ps 77:19-20; Job 9:8.)

11. Can you give a current example of where human traditions may have become more important than doing what is actually expected by God (15:1-11)?

12. In what ways did the Canaanite woman show herself to be not just a person of faith, but more than capable of insisting that Jesus help her daughter (15:21-28)?

Day 5

13. a) Unlike the feeding of the five thousand, Matthew notes that the feeding of the four thousand takes place atop a mountain (15:29). How does this add a special messianic dimension to this later feeding of the masses? (See Isa 25:6-10.)

    b) What other mountaintop experiences in Scripture might add to the appreciation of this scene? (See Exod 19:1-8; Deut 32:49-52; Matt 17:1-2; 28:16-20.)

14. Where in our world is the Church especially challenged to show the compassion of Christ through healing the ill and feeding the hungry (15:32-38)? Where might this apply locally?

15. a) What are the two different events involving Jonah that make up "the sign of Jonah" (16:4)? (See Jonah 2:1; 3:1-10.)

    b) What does each event say as a sign to "an evil and unfaithful generation"? (See 12:39-41.)

Day 6

16. Why do the tensions between Jesus and the Pharisees probably reflect tensions between Matthew's community and the Pharisees (15:1-20; 16:5-12)?

17. a) Why does Jesus confer on Simon the name "Peter" (16:13-20)?

    b) How has the blessing of Peter (16:17-19) affected our understanding of Church leadership through the centuries?

18. If martyrdom is actually the exception rather than the rule, how does following Jesus entail losing one's life for most followers (16:24-25)?

Matthew 17–19

NCBC-NT VOLUME 1, PAGES 90–100

Day 1

1. What in particular stands out to you from last week's lesson (Matt 13–16)?

2. a) In your journey of faith, has the Lord ever taken you to a "mountaintop" experience (17:1-8)? If so, explain.

   b) How have any of your opportunities to glimpse God's glory helped you to recognize God's presence in the day-to-day world?

3. What happens during the transfiguration to tell the disciples that Jesus is more important than Elijah or even Moses (17:1-8)?

Day 2

4. Why was Elijah expected to appear to Israel before the Messiah (17:10-13)? (See Mal 3:23-24.)

5. In Matthew, Jesus urges his followers to use the faith they have, even if it seems "little" in comparison to the task (17:14-20). In what area of your life might Jesus be asking you to do the same?

6. How does the response to Jesus' second prediction of his passion differ from the response his first prediction (16:21-23; 17:22-23)?

Day 3

7. a) What did Jesus teach his followers about payment of the temple tax (17:24-27)? (See Rom 13:5-7 for Paul's view on taxes.)

   b) Occasionally, it is reported that people have refused to pay certain kinds of taxes for reasons of conscience. Is this ever justified?

8. What characteristic of children does Jesus urge his followers to emulate (18:1-5)?

9. What measures has your local faith community taken to protect children from predatory adults (18:6-7)?

Day 4

10. It is not usually our hands or eyes that cause us to sin (18:8-9). What are the causes for sin in your life?

11. a) Have you or a loved one ever been lost (18:12-14)?

    b) If so, describe either the experience of being found or the measures taken to search for the missing one.

12. What are some of the more successful ways you have found to resolve conflicts between people (18:15-17)?

Day 5

13. Does your Bible study group take time through conversational prayer or some other prayer to acknowledge the presence of Jesus in your midst (18:19-20)?

14. a) Have you ever experienced having to forgive someone many times (18:21-22)?

    b) If so, who did it change more, you or the person forgiven?

15. What is the master's motivation for forgiving the servant (18:23-35)?

Day 6

16. Jesus appears to contradict a provision of Mosaic Law that allows for divorce (19:3-9)? What scriptural basis does Jesus use for his teaching concerning the permanency of marriage? (See Deut 24:1-4; Gen 1:27-28; 2:18-24.)

17. In what ways can wealth and possessions be an obstacle to living the gospel message (19:16-21)? (See 6:19-20, also Ps 49:6-10; Luke 12:21; 1 Tim 6:9-10.)

18. What are the rewards in this life and the next for giving up earthly goods and following Jesus (19:27-30)? (See Mark 10:28-30; Luke 18:28-30; 1 Cor 3:21-23; Phil 3:7-8.)

Matthew 20–22

NCBC-NT VOLUME 1, PAGES 100–114

Day 1

1. What event or teaching from Jesus' life covered in last week's lesson has made a particular impression on you?

2. According to the commentary, why was receiving a daily wage of such importance in Jesus' society (20:1-16)?

3. What does the parable of the workers in the vineyard imply about the kingdom of heaven (20:1-16)?

Day 2

4. What information has the third prediction of the passion added to the first and second predictions (20:17-19)? (See 16:21-23; 17:22-23.)

5. In what ways do you see the servant leadership expected by Jesus effectively demonstrated in your faith community (20:20-28)?

6. What evidence is there that the blind men not only had their sight restored, but were given a vision for their lives as well (20:29-34)?

Day 3

7. How does Matthew's use of Zechariah 9:9 give the people's greeting of Jesus special significance (21:1-11)?

8. If Jesus were to visit your parish or home, are there any "tables" he might overturn (21:12-13)?

9. How can the cursing of the fig tree be described as a prophetic action (21:18-22)? (See Jer 8:4-9, 13.)

Day 4

10. How did Jesus' question about John the Baptist set a trap for the chief priests (21:23-27)?

11. After hearing the parable of the two sons and the parable of the tenants and the vineyard, what prevents the priests and the Pharisees from arresting Jesus (21:28-32, 33-46)?

12. a) Has the opportunity to change your mind enriched your life in any way (21:28-32)?

    b) Have you ever rejected a "cornerstone," that is, have you ever turned away something, someone, or some opportunity that you came to regret (21:42)? (See Ps 118:22.)

Day 5

13. Why is there a strong emphasis on proper attire for the wedding feast (22:11-14)? (See 7:21; Rev 19:7-8.)

14. According to the commentary, why is the king's invitation to any and all to attend the wedding feast more shocking than his orders to slaughter those who were originally invited (22:1-14)?

15. Given Jesus' response in 22:17-22, how could some understand Jesus as actually expressing opposition to paying taxes to Caesar? (See Lev 25:23.)

Day 6

16. Carefully read Jesus' response to the Sadducees' question about the resurrection. What tells us that Scripture is to be received as the living word of God (22:31)? (See Exod 3:6, 3:15; 4:5.)

17. If the greatest commandment (22:34-40) is already found in Mosaic Law (see Deut 6:4-9; Lev 19:18), what was so innovative in Jesus' answer to the Pharisees?

18. a) Whose son did the Pharisees say the Messiah was (22:42)?

    b) In Matthew's account, whose son was Jesus suggesting the Messiah was (22:43-46)? (See 8:29; 14:33; 16:16; 27:54, especially 3:16-17; 17:5.)

Matthew 23–25

NCBC-NT VOLUME 1, PAGES 114–127

Day 1

1. What teaching or action of Jesus remains prominent for you from last week's lesson?

2. How might we take Jesus' warnings concerning the hypocrisy of the religious leaders of his time and apply them as a warning against hypocrisy in ourselves (23:1-11)?

3. What would you consider to be important ways that a spiritual leader should serve the needs of others (23:8-12)?

Day 2

4. How might these many woes caution us against embracing a gospel that only promises rewards without warning against the consequences of sin and injustice (23:13-36)? (See 1 Pet 4:17.)

5. Jesus laments over Jerusalem as a mother hen (23:37-39). How does such an image add to your understanding of God? (See Deut 32:11; Ruth 2:12; Ps 17:8; 36:8; 57:2; 61:5.)

6. Why would any talk about the destruction of the Temple (24:1-2) be devastating to faithful Jews? (See Ps 43:3-5; 46:5-8; 48:10; 84:2-3; 132:13-18; Ezek 37:21-28.)

Day 3

7. a) What must happen before "the end" can take place (24:1-14)?

   b) Are there religious sects or denominations in your area that seem preoccupied with the end of the world rapidly approaching?

8. What is meant by the "desolating abomination spoken of through Daniel the prophet" (24:15)? (See Dan 9:27.)

9. a) What image of the "Son of Man" do we find in Dan 7:13-14 to associate with "the sign of the Son of Man" that will appear in heaven? (See also Dan 8:17.)

   b) What are some other images of "the Son of Man"? (See 8:20; Job 25:6; Isa 56:2; Ezek 2:1, 3, 6, 8.)

Day 4

10. If no one can know the day nor hour of the Lord's return (24:36), what is the purpose of stressing his return (24:37-44)? (See 1 Thess 5:1-11; Col 3:3-4; Titus 2:11-14.)

11. How has the liturgical season of Advent assisted you in preparing for the Lord's return (24:36-44)?

12. Apply the parable of the faithful servant to yourself. Where is God calling you to be faithful as you await Christ's return (24:45-51)?

Day 5

13. a) Do only the foolish virgins fall asleep (25:1-13)? (See 26:36-46.)

    b) What distinguishes the wise virgins from the foolish ones?

14. a) The commentary offers a very different interpretation of the parable of the talents, where the master is not seen as a figure for God. If this is the case, what message might have Jesus been giving his followers in this parable (25:14-30)?

    b) The parable of the talents has traditionally been interpreted in a way that sees the giver of the talents as a representative of God. As you read the parable with this understanding, what message does the parable address to you personally?

15. Some of the "sheep" inherit the kingdom by surprise (25:31-46). How does this surprise overturn cultural expectations? You may want to also consider the surprising choices Jesus pronounces "blessed" in the beatitudes (5:1-12).

Day 6

16. Are only those acts of kindness directed towards the king's brothers recognized by the king in the parable (25:31-46)?

17. a) Who are the "least" in your local region (25:40, 45)?

    b) How could this parable of the sheep and the goats be used to encourage ministry to these same people?

18. How does the message in this parable (25:31-46) exemplify Jesus' earlier teaching concerning the greatest commandment (22:36-40)?

Matthew 26–28

NCBC-NT VOLUME 1, PAGES 127–147

Day 1

1. From last week's lesson, what stands out for you concerning Jesus' teachings about his return, the final judgment or the Son of Man?

2. How do the woman's actions with the costly oil cast her in the role of both a prophet and a priest (26:6-13)? (See 1 Sam 16:12-13; 1 Kgs 1:39.)

3. What was Jesus suggesting by saying "the poor you will always have with you" (26:11)?

Day 2

4. Why is it significant that Judas had dipped his hand in a dish with Jesus (26:20-25)? (See Ps 41:10.)

5. What unique element is found in Matthew's account of the cup of the covenant at the Last Supper (26:26-29)? (See Mark 14:23-24; Luke 22:20.)

6. a) What is meant by the "cup" which Jesus prays he will not have to drink (26:36-42)? (See Ps 11:6; 16:5; 23:5; 75:9; 116:13; Isa 51:17, 22; Jer 25:15-16; Ezek 23:31-34; Hab 2:16.)

   b) What are the other cups found in Matthew (10:42; 20:22-23; 23:25-26; 26:27)?

Day 3

7. Jesus prayed that the cup of his suffering might be spared him, but it was not (26:42). Have you ever prayed to be spared a burden, only to discover you had been given the strength to bear it instead?

8. Jesus told the disciple, "Put your sword back into its sheath, for all who take the sword will perish by the sword" (26:52). Can you think of modern examples where passive resistance has helped to positively change history?

9. a) Why was it important at Jesus' trial before the Sanhedrin that there be at least two witnesses against him (26:59-60)? (See Deut 17:6.)

   b) Why is their claim that Jesus said, "I can destroy the temple of God and within three days rebuild it," both false and yet ironically suggestive of the truth (26:59-61)? (See 21:12-13; 24:2; also John 2:19-21.)

Day 4

10. Compare Judas' deep regret for what he had done (27:3) with Peter's response to his denials of Jesus (26:75). Were both responses forms of repentance?

11. Matt 27:25 has sometimes been used to justify anti-Semitism. Why is this inappropriate?

12. Like Simon of Cyrenian, have you ever had to undertake a task you would not have chosen, but which turned out to have redeeming or rewarding aspects (27:32-44)?

Day 5

13. How might Jesus' cry of being forsaken actually be interpreted as a prayer of trust in God (27:46)? (See Ps 22.)

14. a) How does the centurion's response to the earthquake (27:54) contrast with the passersby and the priests and scribes at Jesus' crucifixion (27:39-44)?

    b) Why is it significant that a centurion should respond the way he did? (See 15:24; 28:19-20.)

15. There are some figures mentioned for their care for Jesus just before, after, or during his death, including Simon the Cyrenian (27:32), Joseph of Arimathea (27:57-60), and many women, including Mary Magdalene and Mary the mother of James and Joseph (27:55-56, 61). Whose death or dying have you remembered or attended to in a special way?

Day 6

16. Both the angel and the risen Christ tell the two Marys "do not be afraid!" (28:5, 10). At what times in your life would their words have been most welcomed?

17. How does the risen Christ's commission to the disciples present a major shift in focus concerning what Jesus had taught previously (28:16-20)? (See 10:6; 15:24.)

18. How do you help fulfill Jesus' commission to teach all nations (28:16-20)?

NOTES

ABBREVIATIONS

Books of the Bible

Gen—Genesis
Exod—Exodus
Lev—Leviticus
Num—Numbers
Deut—Deuteronomy
Josh—Joshua
Judg—Judges
Ruth—Ruth
1 Sam—1 Samuel
2 Sam—2 Samuel
1 Kgs—1 Kings
2 Kgs—2 Kings
1 Chr—1 Chronicles
2 Chr—2 Chronicles
Ezra—Ezra
Neh—Nehemiah
Tob—Tobit
Jdt—Judith
Esth—Esther
1 Macc—1 Maccabees
2 Macc—2 Maccabees
Job—Job
Ps(s)—Psalm(s)
Prov—Proverbs
Eccl—Ecclesiastes
Song—Song of Songs
Wis—Wisdom
Sir—Sirach
Isa—Isaiah
Jer—Jeremiah
Lam—Lamentations
Bar—Baruch
Ezek—Ezekiel
Dan—Daniel
Hos—Hosea
Joel—Joel
Amos—Amos

Obad—Obadiah
Jonah—Jonah
Mic—Micah
Nah—Nahum
Hab—Habakkuk
Zeph—Zephaniah
Hag—Haggai
Zech—Zechariah
Mal—Malachi
Matt—Matthew
Mark—Mark
Luke—Luke
John—John
Acts—Acts
Rom—Romans
1 Cor—1 Corinthians
2 Cor—2 Corinthians
Gal—Galatians
Eph—Ephesians
Phil—Philippians
Col—Colossians
1 Thess—1 Thessalonians
2 Thess—2 Thessalonians
1 Tim—1 Timothy
2 Tim—2 Timothy
Titus—Titus
Phlm—Philemon
Heb—Hebrews
Jas—James
1 Pet—1 Peter
2 Pet—2 Peter
1 John—1 John
2 John—2 John
3 John—3 John
Jude—Jude
Rev—Revelation